Becoming an Authorpreneur

A QUICKIE GUIDE FOR MARKETING YOURSELF AND YOUR BOOK

By Susan Barton

For more information about Susan Barton,
please visit ebookreviewgal.com or her author website, at
http://susanbartonauthor.wordpress.com.

Contents

You Are Not Alone

Sounds like the title of a cheesy thriller, right? Well, it can be downright scary to self-publish your book. There are so many things to consider, master and tackle. *Is it okay to self-edit my book? Will I publish only to Amazon? How the heck do I format my file? Should I also create a print copy?* And on and on. Your head was probably spinning.

I won't be going into the answers to those particular questions in this brief marketing guide. I've already covered them in my book, How To Write, Publish and Market Your eBook. This guide is for Indies who've already published their books and need some fresh, new marketing ideas. In this quickie guide, I share several great book-marketing techniques (most of which are free) that you'll be able to put to work today.

You're not alone in this wacky self-publishing world. There are hundreds of thousands of people just like you. Just like you, they decided to self-publish their amazing pearls of wisdom. That can be both a good thing and a bad thing. The upside is you'll often find that many Indies enjoy helping one another. Indie authors who've been through the self-publishing process more than once have become pros at formatting, uploading and networking, and are often happy to give advice to newbies. On the other hand, the downside is there are so many books flooding the market, it's becoming more and more difficult to stand out above all the rest. That's why you need to implement every marketing technique you can think of. A savvy, successful author is one who knows when and how to make the transformation from author to *authorpreneur.*

So, what is an authorpreneur anyway? Well, I'm sure you've heard the word *entrepreneur*. Entrepreneurs are people who invest time and money into a business venture.

When you self-published your book, you made an *investment*. Even if you published your book as economically as possible by taking on the tasks of formatting, editing, creating cover art and uploading your book file on your own – you've still *invested* your *time*. As an authorpreneur, your book *is* your business. As any good entrepreneur knows, a business (aka your book) does not exist in a bubble. It's imperative to get your business message out to the masses. If not, all your hard work will quickly go to waste. This can be said of any business, as well as any book. The clever authorpreneur understands that marketing is critical to any book's success.

From this moment forward, you will need to look at your book as your business. Giving it all the time and attention it deserves will mean the difference between success and failure.

Branding

Just as any good entrepreneur must *brand* himself or herself, authors must do the same. Your brand tells your clients (in this case, your readers) who you are, what you're about and what they can expect from you. Whether you write fiction, non-fiction or both, you should be able to sum up your book and writing style in one or two sentences. In other words, if you had less than one minute to describe yourself and your book how would you do it? Define and refine your brand as concisely and succinctly as possible. For example, my brand would be:

As an author, marketer and entrepreneur, I write about the tips, techniques and tools I've learned over the past two decades. I enjoy sharing these methods with other professionals via my books, articles and custom marketing campaigns.

From there, you might wish to go a step further by creating an easy to remember *tagline*. Take your branding message and whittle it down a bit more. For example, mine would be:

Helping Indie authors succeed by sharing my extensive marketing and entrepreneurial experience.

Your brand should then be utilized across the board. Your website, blog, social media presence, media kit, business cards, postcards, bookmarks, newsletters, email campaigns, etc. should all flow naturally from this branding starting point. Using the same name, logo, profile, photo, tagline, etc., on all platforms will make it much easier for readers, followers and fans to remember and recognize you. You're seeking to establish an emotional connection with your readers. You want readers to eagerly await your next book release.

This is not to say that you are forever bound to your current writing genre. However, it's much easier to brand yourself if your books are of a consistent style. Think of your favorite authors and you'll see how convenient this is. Stephen King is known for his suspenseful thrillers, Michael Connelly is loved for his action-packed detective/crime novels, Nicholas Sparks' literary specialty is heartfelt contemporary romance, and Janet Evanovich's books are a unique blend of comedy, romance and crime. Therefore, you might wish to keep this in mind when planning your next book.

Branding isn't a one-time event by any means. You should continually evaluate and update your image. Keep track of what's working and what isn't working. Spruce things up as necessary.

Your Author Website

I'm assuming you already have an author website. If not, stop what you're doing this moment and get one. You don't have to register a private domain and spend big bucks on a website. Blogger.com and WordPress.com websites are perfectly acceptable platforms. All you need is a valid email address and you're in business. Both Blogger.com and WordPress.com are free and they both include plenty of template options for you to customize and make your website less cookie-cutter-like.

Your author website doesn't have to take you hours and hours to complete, but you do want to spend time perfecting it as much as possible. At a minimum, these basic elements are necessary:

- Attractive header banner (tap into your *brand* here)
- Book purchase links
- Author Bio with photo
- Book Blurb with photo
- Book Reviews

You should also consider adding the following:

- Media Kit
- Video Book Trailer
- Onsite Blog
- Book Excerpt

Your basic website *pages* should include:

- About the Author (your bio and author photo go here)
- About the Book (your book blurb goes here)
- Reviews (add portions of your current book reviews here, or ask for reviewer permission to repost the entire review)
- Contact

Your sidebar area (widgets) is a great place for the following:

- Book Purchase Links
- Social Media Links
- Anything that might not easily fit into a page category (great for those occasional contests, free promos and giveaways)

Once your website is up and running, don't set it and forget it. Remember to update your information as needed. If you've opted for a blog, remember to post regularly. This is a great place to interact with current and potential readers (who can often become reviewers).

Speaking of reviewers, you might want to create a page where you offer review copies of your book. Remember to add a convenient contact form on the page. You can also sell your book via your own website. Create and place a PayPal button so visitors can easily make a purchase.

Get Social

Whether you like the idea or not you're going to have to get social online. Sign up for all the biggies:

Twitter
Facebook
LinkedIn
Google+
Pinterest

Twitter, Facebook and LinkedIn all enable headers. Use this space wisely. As adorable as they might be, it's best not to use photos of your kids and pets as a header. Check the dimensions of each header space (since these vary from site to site) and create an eye-catching header with informational typography. Refer to your branding message and/or tagline.

When posting to social media, remember to maintain the proper balance between self-promotion and interesting engagement. No one wants to read endless posts about how you've written a book and everyone *must* read it. The same goes for personal posts. It's okay to occasionally post about your private life, but do this sparingly. Most of your followers won't be interested in what you ate for lunch or how much you hate Kim Kardashian. In fact, before posting, tweeting or sharing anything you should carefully consider whether it will reflect either negatively or positively on you. Be sure to share plenty of helpful posts as well. Actively seek pertinent information to share. *Retweeting* and *sharing* other users' content is another good way to gain followers. But, again, do this sparingly. Your followers won't appreciate endless threads of regurgitated information.

Just a quick note about buying followers: We've all seen those accounts that promise to provide thousands of "real" followers and fans in exchange for a small amount of money. Resist the urge to do this because:

- These are rarely "real" people

- They won't have a darn thing in common with you and your branding mission
- These lists very often consist of spammers and scammers
- Your time is better spent building *real* relationships with *real* people who will actually buy your book and share your message

Update Your Online Profiles

If you haven't already done so, create an online author profile. Even better, craft a long bio, short bio and two-sentence bio. Not all online profiles are created equal – the amount of characters allowed varies greatly. You'll be glad that you have three variations of your online profile to refer to. Include the most pertinent information, as succinctly as possible. Include direct links to your website, book purchase page and other online profiles whenever possible. Aside from social media profiles, pay particular attention to the following online profile sites:

- About.me
- LinkedIn
- Amazon Author Page
- Goodreads Author Page
- LibraryThing
- AUTHORSdb

LinkedIn, in particular, has tons of options for members to use when crafting a compelling profile. I'm always amazed by how few members take advantage of these features. For example, authors should definitely be taking advantage of the "*Publications*" section. You can add direct URL links and a complete description in this section. Your publications can be just about anything:

- Your books
- Other online profiles
- Online articles
- Websites

In my opinion, every author should be contributing content to *LinkedIn Pulse* (formerly *Pulse News*). You can write about anything, but submitting thoughtful, timely articles is more likely to get your content featured. Always share your published *Pulse* content "publicly" to increase the chances of being featured. Of course, public shares broaden your readership as well. The goal is to reach as many readers as possible, who will then find you so interesting they'll be compelled to check out your expertly written LinkedIn profile.

About.me is a great catchall website for professionals. The profile section allows for a generous amount of information and there are some nice customization options. I've found *About.me* to be quite socially active. The *About.me* community, as a whole, is friendly and encouraging.

Goodreads, *Amazon*, *LibraryThing* and *AUTHORSdb* are geared towards the literary community and are also popular places for readers to visit when searching for more information on their favorite authors and books. Make sure you take full advantage of the profile options on these sites.

Newsletters and Email Campaigns

Once you have followers, fans and website visitors don't let them go. Offer them the opportunity to engage with you on a more personal level via newsletters and special mailings. Sign up with an email marketing service to create monthly newsletters. *MailChimp* is an excellent resource. Place a signup form on your website and share it via social media.

Your newsletters should always include information and opportunities that aren't normally shared elsewhere. You want your subscribers to have a reason to look forward to receiving your newsletters. If it's simply recycled info they can get from your website, or your Twitter or Facebook feed, they'll quickly unsubscribe.

Newsletters are valuable to you because you're certain you're speaking directly to people who want to hear what you have to say – otherwise they wouldn't have subscribed in the first place. Your *return on investment* (ROI) will therefore be much higher than when you toss information out willy-nilly into cyberspace via other marketing vehicles. That's time well spent branding yourself.

Consider including coupons and discount codes in your newsletters. Your subscribers will appreciate receiving special deals on your books and will be more likely to make a purchase – which might very well lead to more book reviews.

Email campaigns can work well too. Just be careful not to overdo it. No one wants to be bombarded with daily emails. If you opt to send out monthly newsletters, then weekly or bi-monthly emails are sufficient. Be sure your emails are necessary, however. If it's information you can withhold until you send out your next newsletter, it's better to wait. The last thing you want to do is annoy your subscribers to the point that they unsubscribe. Last minute promotions and giveaways work well for email marketing. Otherwise, save it for your newsletter.

I can't stress enough how important it is to have permission before sending email and newsletters, otherwise this is spam. That's not the impression you want to make on your current and potential readers.

Help Other Authors

If you position yourself as the go-to resource for other struggling authors, you'll find yourself on the good side of some very important networking connections. Join online groups and contribute often enough to build and maintain your reputation. For instance, *Google+* and *LinkedIn* have hundreds of writing-related groups available. Joining in on popular discussion threads while subtly mentioning your work and experience will quickly produce a valuable network of contacts to draw upon. You could even start your own group, if you have sufficient time to devote to it. However, don't stop there.

You can go a step further by offering to read and review books for other authors, and posting the reviews on your own website. Many authors do this. Interviewing authors and sharing the interviews via your website and social media shows readers how serious you are about this writing business. It also helps keep your readers, followers and fans engaged. After all, you're undoubtedly an interesting person, but there's only so much awesomeness you can share about yourself. Discussing and sharing info about other authors and their books gives you more content to tap into.

Letting other authors know they can depend on you to share their information, news, updates, etc. will make them much more likely to return the favor when the time comes.

Make yourself available to be a book tour or other type of host. Many authors actively seek websites and blogs that share cover reveals, book tours, author spotlights, etc. Letting your fellow authors know you share this content on your site will garner plenty of appreciation that will pay off when you need a favor.

If you don't feel you have enough free time to spend promoting other authors, you can still actively engage with them. Leaving thoughtful and helpful comments on book blogs takes little time, yet gives you the exposure you're looking for since you're often able to include a link to your website in a comment field.

Reviews

I'll start this section by saying DON'T BUY REVIEWS. It's unfair to your readers. It's unfair to authors who play by the rules. And, it's unfair to you. Don't you want to know what people *really* think about your writing and your book? Your writing will most definitely improve and evolve with the help of unbiased constructive criticism.

There's no denying that reviews sell books. Unfortunately, most consumers have become wary of overly positive reviews. Reviews that are nothing but empty praise – *I loved this book! This is the greatest book I've ever read! What an amazingly awesome author!* – are usually discounted and ignored by most potential readers anyway.

You might be thinking, *so if reviews are important and I can't buy them, how am I supposed to get them?* Well, for one you could make sure your book is as close to perfect as possible. Give your readers enough reasons to consider leaving a review and you'll be in business. Keep typos to an absolute minimum (no one is perfect – not even seasoned editors – one or two typos are forgivable). Make sure your book has no formatting issues. If you write fiction, check and double check for consistency and character development.

The truth of the matter is most people who read a book never bother to take the time to write a review. People are busy. They just want to read a book for enjoyment or research and then move on. This is true whether the reader loved the book or hated it. It can often be like pulling teeth to get people to review your book. However, it's still worth the effort to solicit book reviews. Some ideas on how to go about this are:

- Offer free review copies via social media, newsletters, your website, message boards, etc.
- Search online book bloggers and send a polite email.
- Check out *Amazon.com* for consistent, high-profile reviewers and send a polite email.
- Join an author's group via *LinkedIn*, *Goodreads* or other website and carefully solicit reviews.

- Start your own Facebook Book Review Exchange group, website, forum, blog, etc.
- Sponsor a book giveaway contest on *Goodreads* – be aware this is for print copies only and there's no guarantee that winners will review your book.
- Create a specific page on your website, complete with contact form, offering free book copies in exchange for honest reviews.

Don't forget to include a paragraph at the end of your book(s) asking for reviews. It's perfectly acceptable to add something along these lines:

I hope you've enjoyed this book. If so, I'd love it if you'd take just a few minutes out of your busy day to leave a positive review on Amazon and Goodreads. I truly appreciate it!

While you're at it, you can add your author profile at the end of your book as well. Adding an *about the author* allows your readers to know more about you and makes you more approachable.

Go Old School

Print advertising isn't dead. It's very much alive and ready to help you market your book. Authors should take advantage of every new and old school print option available. Utilize things like:

- Postcards
- Bookmarks
- Business Cards

You don't need to spend a lot of money or order through author-specific print shops. Vistaprint is affordable and offers many customizable options for authors. Your local Staples or Office Depot can also be a one-stop printing shop for authors.

Bring your print advertising into the 21st century by adding QR codes to everything. There are many QR code-generating sites where you can insert your URL and have a custom code generated for you. Simply save the QR code as a photo file on your computer and then insert it into your print advertising. Consumers can easily scan your QR code to find out more about you and your book.

Be sure to have a supply of print materials handy at all times. You never know when you'll meet a potential reader or networking contact. Visit local bookstores and other related retailers to ask if they'd be willing to let you leave some cards with them.

Bookmarks should always go out with those all-important review copies. Your readers will appreciate their usefulness and you'll benefit from the free advertising possibilities.

Go Visual

Most of us are busy with our own lives. Many of us have short attention spans. Visual marketing can pack a lot of information into brief, entertaining ads. Consider the following:

Video Book Trailers:

If you've ever gone to the movies, sat through several movie trailers and then were motivated enough to actually see those very movies when they were released you've proven how well trailers work. You can do the same thing with your book.

If done properly, showcasing the most exciting, important and relevant parts of your book with photos, video clips and catchy typography will not only entertain viewers, it will motivate them to buy your book. Search *YouTube* for "video book trailers" and you'll get tons of ideas.

Don't forget to make good use of the "Basic Info" boxes available on *YouTube*. This is where you add all the important information about your book, including direct purchase links, as well as SEO tags (also very important).

Slideshows:

If you have Microsoft PowerPoint, then you have a powerful marketing tool right at your fingertips. Creating an eye-catching, interactive book advertisement in just a few slides is simple. Choose a design (or go minimalist), then add graphics, photos and informational text and you'll have an informative slideshow to add to your website that can be then shared via social media. Not all websites accept PowerPoint files. If that's the case with your website, simply sign up for an account with *SlideShare.net*, upload your file, grab the html code and embed the code on your site. Simple! Just don't forget to add your QR code at the end of your slideshow so potential readers can scan and be taken directly to your website – since a clickable link is not an option with a slideshow.

Infographics:

I LOVE Infographics. They're attractive, informative pieces of advertising that easily fit on one page. Search online for "Infographic templates" and you'll find that several free options will pop up. From there you just fill in the blanks with your own content. You can move things around and add a variety of shapes, graphics, typography and photos. You can wing it as you go along or plan things out ahead of time. Save as a photo and add it just about anywhere.

Sell Sheets:

These one-page promotional sheets were originally meant as handouts for publishers and authors to share with booksellers, retail shops, wholesalers and consumers. Despite what some people will have you believe there is no hard and fast rule regarding what a sell sheet should look like or what information should be included. Aside from your book title, synopsis, cover photo, your bio (with or without author photo) and purchase information, you can be as creative or as simple as you like. Here is my sell sheet for my first book, How To Write, Publish and Market Your eBook, to give you an idea of just how simple, yet effective a sell sheet can be.

Volunteer

This works particularly well if you write non-fiction. You could easily gear your volunteer work towards any number of causes. For example, my second book, *How To Choose, Operate and Market Your Home-Based Business*, is about small business startups. I could easily use my book information to put together a seminar for stay at home moms (SAHMs) and offer to speak to woman's groups in my area. You could do the same thing with your non-fiction book by contacting local organizations to ask if they'd be interested in having you speak at their next meeting or conference. Contacting your local Chamber of Commerce is another option. They can be a treasure trove of valuable leads.

If you write children's books, your options are clear. Volunteering to read to children at your local libraries and schools can be both rewarding and profitable. If you make your book as exciting as possible when reading it to children (practice your drama skills), chances are moms and dads will want to purchase a copy to read to their children at home.

Think about your book's genre and get creative. Some volunteer ideas might be:

- Hospitals
- Church Groups
- Women's Groups
- Book Clubs
- Bookstores
- Libraries
- YMCAs
- Women's and Homeless Shelters
- VA Organizations
- Animal Rescue Centers

Whatever the volunteer vehicle, be sure to bring plenty of copies of your book. You can sell them, give them away or offer a discounted rate. Don't forget those all-important print advertisements. Have plenty of business cards, postcards, bookmarks and sell sheets on hand.

Aside from volunteering to give book readings, you could also donate your time by organizing book drives, coordinating read-a-thons and getting involved in literacy programs. Writing and distributing a press release about the event will garner even more attention for your cause, you and your book. Everyone wins!

Sponsor Giveaways and Contests

Most people enjoy entering contests. Hosting an online giveaway is super simple with *Rafflecopter*. Signup for a *Rafflecopter* account, choose your prize(s) (obviously, your book should be among the prizes), fill out the rest of the info, grab your giveaway code and embed it on your website. Don't forget to share the heck out of your giveaway every chance you get.

If you have a print version of your book, you can sign up for a *Goodreads* book giveaway. These have the potential of attracting hundreds of entrants. *Goodreads* does ask that winners consider reviewing any books they win. Unfortunately, few winners follow through with this. However, if a *Goodreads* contest can result in two or three book reviews it's still worth the effort.

You can also sponsor your own, independent contests. However, it's best to familiarize yourself with all the rules and regulations that go along with this. For example, you're probably aware that you can't ask entrants to purchase anything in order to be entered into your contest. There are other rules you must follow. The Federal Trade Commission (FTC) has very strict rules in place to protect consumers. If you're unsure whether or not your contest adheres to government guidelines you can consult the FTC website.

Think of your giveaway as a promotional means of getting potential readers to find out more about you and your book. Placing the giveaway directly on your author website and then sharing it from there is best. The idea is to give potential readers a reason to visit your website and stick around long enough to check out your book info.

Go On Tour

Familiarize yourself with the Virtual Book Tour process. In a nutshell, a book tour takes you on the virtual road, visiting as many blog sites as possible to increase your book's exposure. You decide when you'd like to begin and end your book tour – a week or two is ideal. Then you choose the content for your tour. This can include reviews, author interviews, character interviews, video book trailers, guest posts and other promotional materials. Finally, you search for, and contact bloggers and website owners, to see if they'd be willing to host you for one day during your tour. There's much more information on the My Book Tour website, http://mybooktour.blogspot.com.

What's great about Virtual Book Tours is you never have to leave your home. Everything is done right from your computer. There's no need to cold call local book retailers. Since your tour stops at several blogs and websites, a Virtual Book Tour has the potential of reaching thousands of visitors, who just might become readers.

In addition, or instead of, approaching bloggers and website owners about participating in your book tour you can gain exposure for your book by offering:

- To be interviewed by the blog owner
- To write a guest post or article
- To give away free books to the first two or three people who leave blog comments relating to your book
- A free book in exchange for an honest review
- To be a host for other bloggers

Virtual Book Tours have become very popular over recent years and tour services have sprung up all over the internet. If you're overwhelmed with the Virtual Book Tour process and decide to hire a service to do all of the work for you be aware that not all services are created equal. Many tour companies offer low-cost services that do not include content creation – they either charge a lot of money to create the tour content or they require that you create your own content. It's never a bargain under these circumstances.

In Conclusion

I have one final piece of marketing advice I'd like to give you. Probably one of the most important things you can do to increase sales is TO WRITE MORE BOOKS. Whether we want to admit it or not, one lonely book on our Amazon Author Page can sometimes cause potential readers to think you decided to give publishing a one-time try and then stopped. Obviously, it takes a while to publish another novel, but why not consider writing a short story or two to add to your list? Short stories sell. They're quick to read and are usually inexpensive. They're also a great way for readers to *try out* a new author. You could even consider offering these as free downloads. The goal with these freebies is to instill confidence in buyers and build your fan base. Having several books listed on your Amazon and Goodreads pages makes you look like the serious writer that you are.

Writing your book might have seemed like the difficult part of being an Indie author. However, the minute you published your book you went from author to marketer and now the *real* work begins. Yet, it doesn't have to overwhelm you. Sit down and write a marketing plan and experiment with different ideas. Take note of what worked and what didn't work. Concentrate on the marketing ideas that have paid off and keep at it.

Book marketing never ends. Unless you hire someone to take over the marketing aspect of your business, you will need to continually stay on top of things. No two books are alike, but many marketing strategies work well for any book genre.

Writing and book marketing is hard work, but it's definitely worth the effort. Happy writing!

Any man who keeps
working is not a failure.
He may not be a great
writer, but if he applies
the old-fashioned
virtues of hard, constant
labor, he'll eventually
make some kind of career
for himself as a writer.'

RAY BRADBURY

About eBook Review Gal and Susan Barton

Susan Barton is an author, book marketer, Indie author coach, copywriter, photographer and artist who enjoys helping other people succeed. Susan's extensive entrepreneurial background has provided her with a wealth of experience to offer Indie authors and other professionals.

If you're overwhelmed by the book marketing process, Susan Barton and her full-service book marketing business eBook Review Gal, at http://ebookreviewgal.com are available to help. Susan offers free and affordable marketing services. Please visit the eBook Review Gal website today to receive a budget-friendly quote to get you started. Susan also offers a variety of Virtual Book Tour services via her My Book Tour website, at http://mybooktour.blogspot.com.

www.ingramcontent.com/pod-product-compliance
Lightning Source LLC
Chambersburg PA
CBHW060445290526
45793CB00002B/588